# Where We Stop to Ponder



Bless Gomes

BookLeaf Publishing

Presentation by *BookLeaf Publishing*

Web: www.bookleafpub.com

E-mail: info@bookleafpub.com

ISBN: 9789357445290

First edition 2021

# DEDICATION

Dedicated to the lovely souls who brought and nurtured the artist within me to take the steps forward and share these pieces of me with the universe and with you.

# ACKNOWLEDGEMENT

The friends and family who always have encouraged me, supported my work, given me their honesty and love through the hardest parts of creating- you made this work come to life and breathe.

# From Memory

Fondness in a moment
Exquisite taste and smells
Messiness in the kitchen
Anticipation for something swell

Laughter and teasing
Hugs and comfort in these arms
Holding me, holding you
The sound of the cooking alarm

Flavors from journeys
Some I've taken, some to be seen
Telling stories to my taste buds
Weaving tales I'll soon dream

A dance and a step
As the evening winds down
And sweet memories we've made
In the time of here and now

# New Horizons

It's not what I expected
It's a different surprise
I smiled from the spark
And the glee that filled up my insides

It's messy and chaotic
I wasn't at all prepared
I realized now all of a sudden
My choices had me scared

I don't even have time to run
Or think, or panic or plan
Please universe, isn't there a sign?
Somewhere, show me if you can

Steady now, steady go
Content and safe in your delight
But if you leave now, in the dark
You'll surely find your light

I'm worried, I'm nervous...
What if it means I've failed?

Listen child, it lead you and shaped you,
You're prepared now, so sail.

# Taal

I woke up before a dawn
To the sounds of early rain
It wasn't time to arise
Yet my body could not just stay

Tiptoeing in the silence of the hour
No soul awake
The floorboards sighing with my soft steps
I felt my way to the light outside

I held my breath
Expecting nothing
And the sky shuddered
Surrendering the captive drops onto my skin
Waking me up from the dream within

And I woke up on a pillow
To the sound of the rain
the smell of the earth and sky
Lingering in my hair

The touch of the grass under my palms
Kissed by the clouds
Humming to myself as I reveled
In the sounds of the earth come alive again

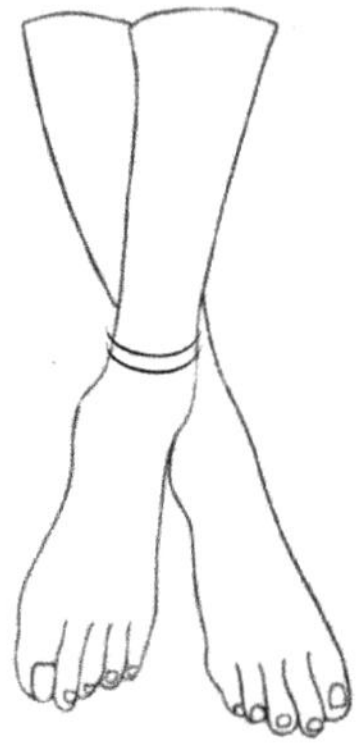

# Infatuation

Many lovers, many moons
I felt it before.
I breathed into the night air, remembering the familiar feelings

I sighed, wondering when inevitably it too, would go.

Then came upon my path, a whisper into the night
I couldn't run from it, I didn't want to
I followed, I watched.
I longed to hold it close.

It found me first, and I wanted it to last
Please stay, I thought, please don't leave again
With a gentle smile, a small sigh
Asks me, "won't you stay this time?"

# Discovering

Isn't it funny
When I searched for you
I found more of me instead

When I looked every corner
When I listened between the pulses
And I found something of mine
Yet I didn't recall putting it there

And every piece showed me
That I wasn't searching for a way to get you back
Not a way to find you again

I'd lost me so many times
I'd forgotten where I was
I couldn't see the layers anymore
Who had I become?

I wasn't a half to begin with
Yet all the pieces I found
Made me begin to think
I'd started to only be half of who I am

And I'd thank you if I could
But I think it's enough now
To know I'm whole always

To find more of me growing where I'd forgotten I could bloom

# What Might Be

Wonder and wonder
How softly your voice murmurs
Sleepily
On my skin

How tempting
To leave a kiss
Morning dew
But on smiling lips

Fingers
Holding mine
Small hands
Nestled in
Lines and creases
Little pathways

Perhaps our stories
Written along the ways

A little touch
Of gentle days

# Trying

Will you allow me to show you this light
A little weak
But trying to burn with a little bit of bright
It can't serve you more than it can serve me
But won't you come look
Won't you come and capture it with your eyes
With a mind accustomed to the darkness
The mind that doesn't fear it
But the mind that can't fathom it
Will you shy away
Before you muster up the urge to look
To allow it to claim you
A tiny part of your memory
The forgotten sense buried away
A spectacle that seems so ordinary
Yet you sit here in awe
In the reflection of a little light
That lasts no more than now

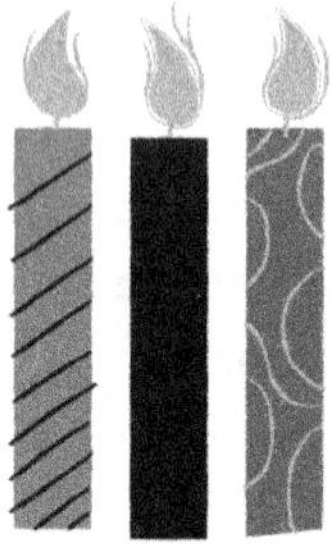

# Taking the Risk

I opened up my heart
While holding Fear's hand
Walking somewhere
Unknown and familiar
A strange, captivating land

I wandered a bit ahead
tasted the freedom, made a wish
Around me the land changed
Sparkling, shining, a calm in my steps

In the land I soon forgot-
the fear I so carefully held onto,
That hesitation that once kept me safe,
But in the safety of Fear and it's grasp
I missed the oasis of this space

And once my feet met the stars
Lighting my journey of a million days
Love found my hand and walked with me,
Accompanying me on my way

# A different kind of medicine.

Not the kind that surges in your veins for a bit and leaves you
Not the kind that runs through your circuits
Not the kind that leaves me restless when it's in my system,
But leaves me more restless when it's not

I need the kind I can make myself
And when I can't, I can find it

In unexpected places
When I didn't know I needed it most
When it finds me anyways
In friends and places
Between pages and notes
Messy ink and neat lines
Gentle rhythms, booming bass
Silky sheets or heavy blankets

I need that kind of medicine
Dancing on my tongue
Whispering in my ears
Tiptoeing on my skin
Waking me into another dream

The kind that isn't in a bottle
Or pill, or drink
That can't be manufactured
That comes with more than just a fleeting feeling
And keeps me blooming

# The Next

I ask for more
But never for too much
I'm out of luck
I tried not to rush

One ticket please
For the train to somewhere
I can't be late
I must take myself
With haste, with care

I'm running now
Must catch this car
Faster yet, I go
But it's going so far

Oh wait, oh why?
It's where I must go
I'm slipping, sliding
No one seems to know

Someone catch me
Oh please, can you hear my voice
I'm frantic, I'm worried
I have only a moment's choice

The train to somewhere has left

But I hadn't bound it in time
Everything was going
Yet somehow I missed a line

Now what I can I do
It's no use making a fuss
I'm too weary for the next train
Yet a plan was a must

I must gather myself now
Another train must be on its way-
But what if it leaves me again?
Is it wrong of me to say?

And soon enough it's here-
A train to somewhere returns
I'm nervous but this time I'll board,
Not asking much, just as before
But this time when I'm on the train
I'll hope just a little bit more

# Starting the Day

If I wait a few more moments
I'll trade the warmth that tempts me
Give into the smells that tickle my nose,
Rising from the kitchen
Stirring a wake up to my belly

If I reach over the pillow
And close my eyes again
I'll hear the clutter of spoons and cups
The chorus of chittering and chirps
The occasional rattle of the door that's loose

But if I take the notebook near me
And pick up the pen inside
Where will the ink lead me
Is it something I can tell the pages to confide?

I suppose the answers await
So long as my curiosity holds
And for now I'll do that
To follow the day that unfolds

# Sweet Fruit

Day by day
Sun tender
Kissed gently
Held in familiar hands

“You who have not ripened,
Sweetness will come with time,
But until you leave this garden,
I will hold you in these hands of mine.”

Night by night
Some fall, some sway
Even those upon the ground
Feeding the curious and hungry wanderers

“The time has come,
From your safe branch I’ve taken you,
To your purpose not so different from the rest.
Feed and nourish the one who chooses you,
As the ones you grew with did too.”

# The Middle of Things

A flutter
it came to surprise me
the feeling welling up
almost like tears

But I'm not sad
as I'm holding my breath
the exhale slipping
as I contemplate what it is

Is it a passing infatuation
residing in this small space
a time that is a "here"
and a "now" to cherish

Maybe it was a passing glance
that brought me back
a second look
that turned over everything I expected

For now I don't know
one day I'm sure I'll have the answers
and be able to catch the moment
when the road is clear

And til that moment

I'll savor the time
the chapters and story
when it was almost mine.

# Sakura

Pinks and white
My heart delights
A wonder of petals in the air
Cascading down in a flowery snowfall
Brushing my finger, softer than a silk sheet
The lightest of fragrance
Yet heaviest of warmth
A season too fast, too soon
Too short to keep in forever bloom

# Breaking Through

Forged in heat
Tested in fire
It will strengthen you
Mightier than the first form

I'm melting
I'm mixing
The experiences color me
Like the metals that enforce the blade

I can carry the weight now
Has it gotten lighter than before?
You've grown stronger
You can push harder now

I will get hurt
But I can endure it
I'm stronger now
My experience to shield me
My resolve to defend me

Push until it breaks
Push until you breakthrough

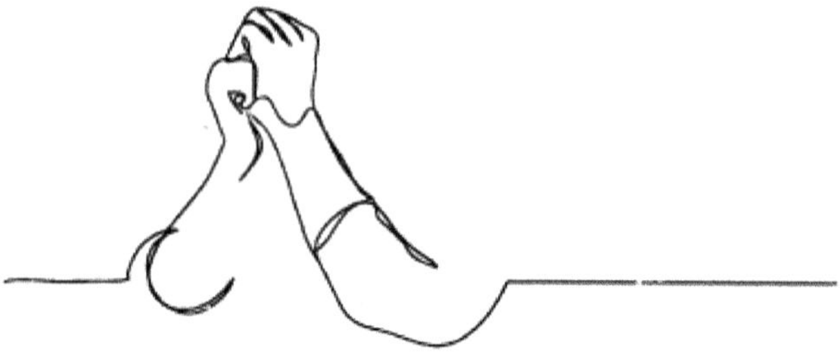

# Familiar.

Was it
the sound of your voice
the crease in your cheek
a light in your eyes
that made me wonder

As I watched in awe
the revelry unfolded
a moment of bliss

A carefree glance
across the way
the familiar spark
of two who have met before

# Submerged

A last inhale before I sink
A slow exhale into a dream
Inch by inch the dryness succumbs
The gentle, waving beckoning lulling me under

How long ago did I go
I've lost the sense of what I called time
A haze covers my eyes with its nimble fingers

I don't struggle
I can't see
Yet in the vastness I can feel the bottom
Something pulsing
Something racing with my own tempo
The entity holds me close as it pushes me to break the surface

A sensation stirring in my fingertips
Release your tension, let go of your pains
Shoulders at ease
Though my chest grows tighter
There's no fear here

# A Dream

I'm floating in somewhere
Every time I let go
I'm lost again and I'm looking
Next time, I won't let go

I'm pulled back to earth
I'm wrapped in this embrace
It's sunshine and warmth
It's radiating on your face

I don't want to fall back asleep
What if I won't get to stay
My eyes protest
My heart urges a little more
One word, two words
Each lighting up my night sky

Will we be here tomorrow?
Every second passes in anticipation
I reach out, but I'm floating again

I don't want to drift alone again
Can I fight it down to earth?
I toss, I turn, I struggle and tire
Til I see you're here, floating in the mirth

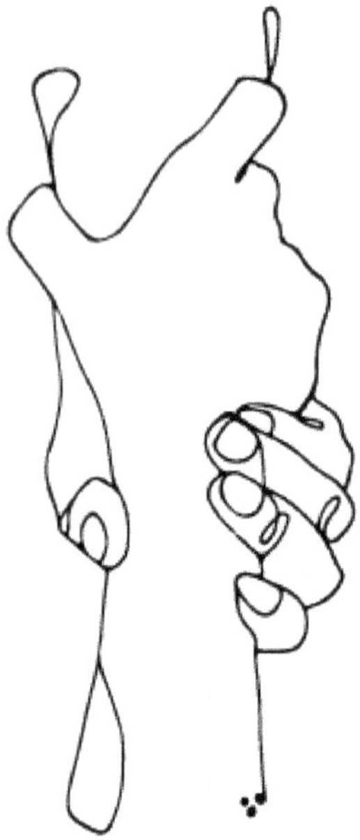

# A kind of love...

The kind of love
That melts my heart
That leaves wrinkles in my cheeks
From endless smiles
And laughter
That sparkle that lives
In my eyes
When I think of you
When I hold you tight
The sound when you inhale
And drink in my thoughts
When I have no more to say
When I'm lost for words

The kind of love
That stirs in my soul
That plays a melody on my heartstrings
That carries me on a frequency
Holding me gently
Resting in the waves

# Reminiscent

I let go of the petals
That fell into my hands
Their soft and fragile skin
Resting for but a moment

I relished that sensation
Like gentle hands meeting
Wanting to hold and to feel,
The same warm palms pressed on mine

I closed my eyes and imagined
The touch of your skin
Faintly, carefully
Locking our fingers as one

I pined by the water
And wished on a star
The moon creeping out for company
Trying to fill where you are

# A Pause in Time

When your smile touches your eyes
The stillness of then, caught between each sigh
I want to reach over
And borrow a moment from time
Play it over and over again
The gentleness in two hearts
A meeting of the ages

Held in warm arms
Indescribable to just a few pages
A chapter none wants to end

www.ingramcontent.com/pod-product-compliance
Lightning Source LLC
Chambersburg PA
CBHW051743130826
49812CB00033B/981
*9789357445290*